THE VISION BOARD BOOK

Create Your Vision Board in a Book: Envision What You Want and Get It

by Gini Graham Scott, Ph.D.

Author of *Mind Power: Picture Your Way to Success*, *The Empowered Mind: Harness the Creative Force Within You*, and *Want It, See It, Get It!*

THE VISION BOARD BOOK

Copyright © 2017 by Gini Graham Scott

TABLE OF CONTENTS

CHAPTER 1: WHY CREATE A VISION BOARD IN A BOOK? 4

CHAPTER 2: WHY CREATE A VISION BOARD? 7

Gaining Clarity...7

Experiencing Focus and Concentration 8

Being Motivated...9

Why a Vision Board Works So Well 9

Changing Your Vision 10

CHAPTER 3: DECIDING ON YOUR GOALS 11

CHAPTER 4: USING VISUALIZATION TO DECIDE WHAT YOU WANT 17

The Power of Visualization 17

How to Visualize...18

CHAPTER 5: CREATING YOUR VISION BOARD BOOK 21

How to Make Your Vision Book 21

ABOUT THE AUTHOR 93

CHAPTER 1: WHY CREATE A VISION BOARD IN A BOOK?

Usually a vision board consists of a large white board about 24" x 36," and you fill it up with illustrations and photos which express your hopes and dreams. As you create it, you may think about, meditate on, and visualize what you hope to achieve, using these images to make your vision more graphic and dramatic. Later, you might post your vision board in a place where you can see it often to remind yourself of what you want, which can help you make your vision a reality.

Now you can create your vision board in a book. The advantage of this approach is that you can take this book with you wherever you go and look at it whenever you want. You can also readily share this book with others, and you can take a photo of the pages or turn your book into a PDF and share that, too. Plus, with a book you can add in comments, add pages, and otherwise expand on your original vision. It is also easier to store and carry around.

In fact, you can readily create a series of vision boards every year or every few months, so you can both see where you are going and where you have been.

Perhaps think of this book like a visual journal or diary in which you record your hopes and dreams and later look back from time to time. But now you have a separate book which you can focus on each day and use to keep track of how you are doing, as well as motivate you to go after and make real what you want.

For that's the thing about visions.   Like any goal, purpose, mission statement, or future you can imagine, you have to take steps to make it real. The initial vision helps to display very clearly what you want for yourself and who you want to become. Then, you have to take steps to make that vision come alive. Consider the vision like a bright light lying ahead of you promising all sorts of possible rewards for you achievement. But you have to take the steps to go towards that light, like any destination. And you don't get the rewards until you get there.

This book is designed to get you started. Later, you can create your own vision book with as many pages as you want.   So now, go forward. Create your vision in this book. Then, map out the steps you will take to make that happen in the last section of the book.

CHAPTER 2: WHY CREATE A VISION BOARD?

If you have already created a vision board, you know the whys and wherefores of creating one. If you haven't already created one or want a refresher on the purpose of doing this, three key reasons for doing this are gaining:
- Clarity
- Focus and concentration
- Motivation

Gaining Clarity

You gain clarify because a vision board helps to make your life goals or your goals for the next few months or year clearer. Also, a vision board can clarify how you might want to change yourself. It can help you clearly state what you want or think is best for you now.

The images you choose can help you gain this clarity by showing you graphically what you most desire. For example, if you imagine that you want a better life or more success in your work that is overly general. So your board can help you clarify what your definition of a better life or success means to you, such as if you want a new car, a new home, a more fulfilling relationship, more money, a more outgoing personality, or a more attractive appearance to appeal to others.

As you visualize your goals and gather images to express these ideas that will help you clarify what you really want. The reason for using images is that you will typically be inspired to pick certain images because you connect with them emotionally rather than trying to reason out what you goals should be.

For further clarification, as you imagine these goals and gather images to represent them, ask yourself why you want a particular result. The "why" will help you understand your reason for choosing this goal, which will give you more incentive to move towards achieving it.

For example, do you want more money for security? Or do you want it to get a bigger house and more expensive car, and if so, why? Is that because these images of success will open up new connections and possibilities for you, so you can realize your dream of developing new creative projects, because you see this money as a sign of success, or because you feel you will gain more recognition and prestige by living a more affluent life style. Or maybe you are inspired by a combination of these things, or something else. Drill down to learn your underlying reasons for why you want something.

Whatever your "why," think about what is the "why" or "whys" for you. You can find your "why" if you keep asking yourself the question: "Why do I want that?" Or get relaxed and visualize as you ask yourself this question and let the answer come to you.

Gaining this clarity of what you want and why will help you be more focused on this goal, as well as be more motivated to do what it takes to get it.

Experiencing Focus and Concentration

Secondly, a vision board can help you become more focused, since you now know what you want and why. As a result, you can keep this goal – or the several goals expressed on your board in front of you. If you have multiple goals, decide on the one or two most important goals to go after first, since otherwise you will be too scattered. You want to prioritize what you want to get, so you can concentrate your energy on fully achieving that one thing – or in some cases, those two things, if you can manage to do both at the same time.

The use of images to show what you want helps you keep that focus, since the images are a graphic reminder, which you can see each day or several times a day to remind you of your goal. These regular reminders can help you take some steps each day to achieving this goal. Even if other things come up which you have to attend to first, you still will get that reminder to work towards your goal as soon as you can. Another advantage of these images is they remind you not only of your goal, but the steps to take to make it a reality.

Being Motivated

Once you know your goal or goals and why, your vision board will help you stay motivated to get there.

Consider your goal like the destination you are driving to in your car and your why like the fuel or energy you need to get there. Your focus is the clear path on the road ahead. And your motivation is you as the driver stepping on the gas. The more you step on it, the faster you will go, because you have even more motivation to get to your destination even more quickly.

To increase your motivation even more, add affirmations and motivational quotes to your board that inspire you to keep going, a little like listening to uplifting messages or songs as you drive along. You might add in success stories that help to show what's possible, which is akin to listening to such stories on the radio or on a DVD while you drive. These additions to your board likewise help to keep your enthusiasm and excitement high, so you are even more motivated to work towards getting what you want.

Why a Vision Board Works So Well

A vision board works so well because of the power of the images and any short affirmations, motivational messages, or stories you put up there. In placing any text, think of it as being a short word balloon or tweet, so it has maximum visual impact. You want to look at it and quickly get the message.

Likewise, posting strong images which you gather from magazines, photos, illustrations, online websites, and other sources can highlight your goal and make it stand out very dramatically, so it is memorable. These images are like seeing the trailer for a film, in which the key points play out so you want to see that film. Likewise, strong powerful images will inspire you to work towards the goal, so you can see it through to the ending, just like going to see a compelling film.

Or consider yourself imagining where you want to go on a vacation. You think of different places you might go and imagine yourself there.

In short, your vision board works so well because it serves as a graphic reminder of what you want. Then, the additional clarity, focus, and motivation it provides helps to propel you to work towards what you want, so you achieve your goals even more quickly.

Changing Your Vision

While you want to work towards achieving a particular goal or goals based on the vision board you have created, over time your goals can change, as you achieve what you want and are ready to work towards something new.

When that happens, be ready to create a new vision board to reflect your new vision. Then, go through the same process to create your board and use it as a day to day reminder of what you want and what you are going to do to achieve it.

CHAPTER 3: DECIDING ON YOUR GOALS

You can create a vision board to achieve all kinds of goals. Different people have different priorities, ranging from work, business, and wealth to personal development, relationships, and family. It all depends on what you want at this stage in your life.

While it is best to focus on achieving one or two goals that are of the highest priority, these can be complementary goals in different spheres of your life, while other goals can be waiting in the wings. This way after you achieve one goal, another goal takes its place.

You might imagine this choice like casting a theatrical or film production. The best productions have one or two leads that everyone can most closely identify with, as the play or film focuses on one or two stories. The rest of the characters play supporting roles, though in future productions, a formerly supporting actor may take over a lead role, or a spin-off may feature that actor. Meanwhile, the story line with the original lead has concluded, so the story moves on to feature someone new. By the same token, your main goals may give way to other goals as they are successfully achieved and concluded.

As for complementary goals, one approach is to have one primary goal for your work or business life and another for your personal life, while other goals that are less important for now can come from either arena. Consider them like subgoals or goals in waiting. But you will generally get images for each of your goals, though if you prefer, you can get images for your most important goals first.

The major goals to think about include these major areas:

Work or career: What sort of job or business do you want? Where will it be? What do you need to be successful, such as a certain level of sales or a promotion?

Personal development: What do you want to change or improve in your personal life? Is there anything about your personality you would like to be different? Do you have any fears to overcome? Do you feel any personal conflicts about who you are or what you should do to resolve those issues?

Clothing: Are you eager to make a change? Do you want new clothes to express the new you? Might fashion appeal to you as a new career? You can put this on your vision board, too.

Health and fitness: Is there anything you need to do to be healthier? Do you want to eat a healthier diet? Do you want to lose weight? Do you want to give up smoking or drinking? Do you want to stay fit or become fitter by doing more exercise yourself or joining a gym or fitness class?

Relationships: Is there anything you want to change here? Do you want to find a relationship or improve one you are already in? Do you feel a need to break up a current relationship and want to figure out the best way to do it? Is there anything you need to change about yourself or your expectations, so things will go more smoothly in finding or being in a relationship?

Family: Is there anything you want to do differently in dealing with your parents, kids, or relatives? What are your goals or plans for what to do with members of your family?

My house: Are you thinking of moving? Do you want to live in a bigger house? Do you want to move to another town, county, or state? Or do you want to change something in your house, such as redecorating, remodeling, or moving furniture around? Do you want to turn one room into an office, and what should that look like? You can also imagine different outcomes on your vision board.

Money: What are your goals for making or obtaining more money? Do you want more income from your job or business? Do you want to make more money as an investor in different properties or projects? Do you have any fears or insecurities about money that you want to overcome?

Fame or reputation: Are you seeking to become known or famous in your field or in your community or beyond that? What might you do to increase you44r visibility and credibility? Do you need to gain more confidence? Do you want more opportunities speaking to groups and organizations?

Travel and vacations: Is there some place or places you would like to go? Do you want to take a special kind of trip, from climbing a mountain to relaxing on a beach in the tropics? How would you like to spend your next vacation?

Adventure: Do you want to do something exciting? Do you want to participate in some adventurous activity, such as rock climbing or bungee jumping? Would you like to reward your hard work with something out of the ordinary? Envisioning what you want to do can help to make that happen.

Gaining knowledge: Is there something you want to learn about, whether for your job or business or for your general knowledge about history, art, music, science, or other cultures? Do you want to understand more about psychology? Is there someplace you want to go to take courses to learn more?

Spiritual or religious connection: Do you want to develop a deeper connection to God? Do you seek a closer relationship with nature? Do you yearn for a greater sense of purpose in life? Whether you feel more drawn to becoming more spiritual in general or becoming more committed to a particular religious path, you can seek a greater sense of spirituality or faith with a vision board.

Participating in social activities and causes: Are you interested in getting involved in social activities, in your community, or changing the world to make it a better place? Does local or national activism appeal to you? Is there a cause that inspires you? Again, your vision board can help to guide you in that direction.

Anything else? What else might you want? You can put just about anything on your board, from the latest tech items or gadgets to world peace.

15

The above listing of ideas are suggestions to get you started, so feel free to envision whatever you want. You can also use your vision board to dream, fantasize, and let your imagination soar to create your visions just for fun.

But most importantly, your vision board should feature your wants and dreams which can really happen. These are what are known as SMART goals, which stands for goals which are Specific, Measurable, Achievable or Attainable, Realistic, and Time bound. As such, you can use your vision board as a form of task management in which you decide on the most important tasks to do, determine how to do them, and focus on achieving them within a certain time frame.

Say you want to start a new business. Your Specific goal is to identify what kind of business. The goal becomes Measurable when you indicate what it will cost to start that business. It is Achievable if you have the skills to organize and run that business. It is Realistic if you have the money or a way to get the funds needed, such as through friends, family, or a bank loan. And it's Time-bound if you set up a schedule to take the steps to get the funds and obtain the resources you need, including the location for operating the business.

Once you identify your SMART goal, create a plan to initiate the steps to make that goal happen. At the same time, set up a way to document what you have done and the results, so you stay on track to achieve your goal.

Along the way, keep looking at your vision board regularly to remind yourself of where you are going, which will help you stay motivated to keep working towards your dream. If circumstances change, be ready to change your plans, and as needed modify your dreams, for you can always create a new vision board – or you can modify the pages in your vision board. This way, you can consider your board like a living, breathing document that helps to guide you where you want to go and lets you change direction as needed.

CHAPTER 4: USING VISUALIZATION TO DECIDE WHAT YOU WANT

The Power of Visualization

In deciding on your goals, before you construct your board, use visualization to help you imagine even more powerfully what you want to do. Some people like to think through things rationally, which is fine if you prefer to make your choice that way. But ideally, try to set your rational mind aside so you can see more graphically what you want to do. Using visualization will help you feel more emotionally invested, connected, and motivated to do whatever you come up with.

You might imagine the difference in using visualization versus rational thinking as the difference between reading something on a page and seeing something in a movie or video. Today, video is becoming more and more popular as the way to share anything, whether on Facebook, Twitter, Instagram, or in the movies. That's because seeing a story or event is much more powerful than only reading or hearing about it. Visualization is like that film experience, except that you are creating your own video or movie in your mind's eye, as you imagine what you want and how to get it.

These images or the movie in your mind make whatever you are imagining more real. And the more you see something, the more power it has to inspire and motivate you to act to make that happen in reality – just as the more you think about something you want, the more you want to work towards making it happen. Accordingly, visualization is more powerful in motivating you to take action to make what you see real.

By the same token, when you find images and short text statements to reflect what you are visualizing, that helps to reinforce your goal and the actions you are taking to get there.

How to Visualize

There are a number of ways to visualize, but basically you want to get very comfortable and relaxed. It's best to find a quiet place in your home, office, or natural setting. If it helps, turn on some soothing music to relax you, or if you prefer, be in a quiet environment to do this. That's my preference, although when I first learned to visualize, the leader put on some soft background music, though I found that distracting.

As you move from one state of consciousness to another, you might use a countdown, such as used in hypnosis to get someone into a relaxed hypnotic state and later bring them back. For instance, you can get into an altered intuitive state by saying to yourself words like "You are getting more and more relaxed; more and more relaxed. And as I count from 1 to 5, you are getting more and more relaxed, more and more relaxed, yet staying awake and aware. 1…2…getting even more relaxed…3…4…5." Alternatively, when it's time to return to everyday consciousness, you go in the other direction, saying something like: "And now you are becoming more and more alert, more and more alert. And as I count from 5 to 1, you are getting more and more alert, more and more alert. 5…4…getting more and more alert…3…2…even more alert…And now 1, you are back in the room and back to your normal consciousness."

However you do it, quickly put yourself into a more intuitive altered state of mind, where you can readily see things, even with your eyes open. As you regularly visualize, you will need less prep time to get ready. You can almost immediately turn on this intuitive part of yourself, as I learned to do after a couple

18

of years of working with visualization and intuition, although I started out initially closing my eye, getting relaxed, and letting my intuition lead the way.

Once you are in this relaxed state, ask yourself a few questions, one at a time; then let your intuitive right brain take over. Don't try to think of your answers. Instead, let the answers come to you.

For most people, these answers can come in a visual form, where you see the answers on your mental screen like a movie in your mind. Or you may experience the answers as a voice in your head speaking to you or as thoughts that go through your mind. Sometimes you may get a feeling or sense of knowing the answer.

These four types of responses are related to whether you are more likely to get your information in a visual or auditory form, or whether you are more of a feeler or knower, as I experienced in a group on visualization techniques, after we were led in a visualization experience. We were put in different groups based on our primary mode of perception – visual, auditory, feeling, or knowing, designed to show everyone how each group got their answers differently. Yet, while one mode will be stronger for you, we all have a little of each mode of perception, and you can work on increasing any of your perceptual abilities.

For the purpose of creating your vision board, it's preferable to visualize as much as possible, although if you get your information in the form of thoughts, use that mode. Feelings and knowings are fine to reinforce an insight you have gained from visualizing, so you feel more sure that's what you should do. But otherwise, feelings and knowings are less useful for this process. So ideally, as you ask your questions, see things in your mind's eye, since that will guide you in selecting images for your vision board.

If you want, write down what you see as your answers or say them aloud and record them with a recorder or the voice app on your phone. Then, from memory or what you wrote down or recorded, start gathering things for your vision board.

You can use your smartphone to take photos which you can later print and crop to any size for your board. You can also get stock photos to print for your board through stock photo houses. The three I use the most are www.adobestock.com, www.123rf.com, and www.istockphoto.com. If you have a choice of sizes, select photos with at least a 300 dpi (dots per inch) resolution – the recommended minimum size for printing. The cost is $1 to $3 for most images.

The second half of this book is divided up into these 12 sections corresponding to the different types of goals you might have. Each one consists of three pages, where you can paste or tape in different photos, illustrations, or text. Use the results of your visualization to guide you in what to collect. You can use whichever sections you want for your vision board. Just keep the images you have seen or the voices or thoughts you have experienced in mind as you find material for it. Also, consider those images as a starting point to get you going, and be ready to look for other ideas and images as you go along.

Using visualization is a great way to start the process, much like using brainstorming. It opens up the door to your creativity with some images to get you started. Then, let your imagination go as you collect images to express your goal and the actions you need to take to get there. Often you may experience a relaxed, dreamlike state as you gather your materials, which is akin to visualizing with your eyes open. Often, too, when you get started with visualization, you need this kind of warm-up to start visualizing in response to a topic or question. But once you gather the materials, you are already warmed up, so you are better able to visualize what fits or doesn't fit on your board as you go.

In sum, get ready to start visualizing and see what images come to you. Keep going as long as the images keep coming. As they stop, you might ask yourself one last time, "Is there anything else I should want or do to achieve my goal" and see what comes. After no more images come, stop the process and return to your everyday reality.

Now happy visualizing and setting your goals.

CHAPTER 5: CREATING YOUR VISION BOARD BOOK

Once you have imagined what you want and visualized possibilities, you are ready to create your vision board book. This is the same as creating a vision board, except instead of creating it on a large white board, you are creating it in a book.

You can use the pages in the second half of this book to do this, and if you prefer, you can remove these pages to create your own separate book. You can use an X-Acto or other sharp knife to do this. Though there's already a cover with the title "My Vision Book," you can create your own cover and title it whatever you want. Add the date you have created this. When you create another book or books, you can add these dates and start a series of vision board books.

Later, you can think of any of your vision books as a reminder of your goals and hopes and plans for achieving them. You can share your book with others, too, such as if you are in Vision Board Book support group – or any other kind of support group. You can also scan the pages to create a PDF to share with others. You can even turn your PDF into a published book, such as by using Amazon's CreateSpace platform (www.createspace.com), so you can share your Vision Board book or books even more widely.

How to Make Your Vision Book

To start creating your book, find a place in your home or office where you will be undisturbed. It could be the same place you used for visualizing your goals and achieving them, or it could be some place where you have a table or desk, so you can lay out the materials you will use to create your book.

If you want to use images from your computer, website, or online search, sit near your computer, laptop, or smartphone and have a printer nearby to print the images you obtain.

More specifically, the materials to make your book get the following:

- Magazines or other materials with images you can cut up.

- Optionally, set up a computer with website access and a printer to find online images and print them.

- Scissors or a sharp knife, such as an X-Acto knife, to cut out images or trim those you print on your printer.

- Glue, Scotch tape, or masking tape to paste your images into the Vision Board Book.

Then, in a focused, even meditative state, look for images that reflect the goals you want to achieve in each category. Later, you will prioritize what you want to do first, but for now, just select whatever images you feel drawn to.

Print out any images you find online or on your computer, laptop, phone, and trim them to feature the image you have selected. Get rid of any extraneous borders or trim away any images you don't want, such as if you want to select a person from a group shot or want to highlight a product that is part of a display. Likewise, crop any pictures from magazines or other written materials if you want to highlight a particular image.

Initially, you might choose pictures randomly, based on whatever appeals to you. But then select those pictures you feel most closely reflect your goal or goals.

Use the listed categories as a guide to selecting pictures, though add your own categories if you want. After you select the images for a particular category, apply some glue or tape to the back of the picture and place in on the page. In using tape, you can fold it over, so one side is on the picture, the other on the page.

Place the images quickly, as you respond to them, so you make these placements more intuitively and spontaneously, rather than thinking carefully about what to place and where. A vision board is not designed to be a piece of art – rather you are placing the images as you respond to them to reflect what you most want – and what you plan to do to achieve that result.

If you later want to move an image or find that some images you have selected don't fit or you want to trim an image to better position it, you can do so. In this case, an advantage of initially taping the image to the page is that you can later move the image to place it somewhere else. Later, you can always glue it permanently in place. In general, though, it's best to go with your initial placement rather than trying to move images around and arrange them later. The first placement is more spontaneous and intuitive, so it more accurately reflects what you are thinking and feeling at the time.

While you can arrange the images on your board however you want, try to place them to emphasize the ones you feel are most important or have the highest priority for you. To do so, place these images in the top center or middle of the page or use larger images, so they dominate the page. Then, place the other images to either side or lower down on the page. This way your most important priority images are like headlines on top or in the center of a bullseye in the middle of the page – like a target used in archery practice.

In a regular vision board, the usual practice is to put your most important goals and the images representing them in the center and place less important goals and images spreading out in any direction. This process is a little like creating a mind map, with the branches radiating out from the center. But in creating a vision board book, you have limited space to place multiple images, so you might put your less important goals and images on a second, third, and even more pages. This way the first page in a category is your most important goal; the second page, your next most important goal, and so on. If a particular type of goal isn't important to you now, leave that category blank.

Feel free to cut the following pages out of this book to create your own vision book, which you can look at whenever you want as a reminder. You can also share it with others or scan it into a PDF to post on a website or send to others. You can additionally rearrange the pages if desired to put your highest priority visions first, as well as drop any categories where you don't have any goals and images. Finally, you can copy the original pages to use them again and again as you create new vision books with new visions.

MY VISION BOOK
Date:_____

WORK OR CAREER

Add your images here and on the next page.

PERSONAL DEVELOPMENT

Add your images here and on the next page.

CLOTHING

Add your images here and on the next page.

HEALTH AND FITNESS

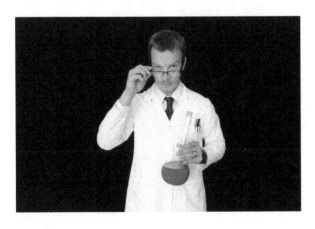

Add your images here and on the next page.

RELATIONSHIPS

Add your images here and on the next page.

FAMILY

Add your images here and on the next page.

MY HOUSE

Add your images here and on the next page.

MONEY

Add your images here and on the next page.

FAME OR REPUTATION

Add your images here and on the next page.

TRAVEL
AND VACATIONS

Add your images here and on the next page.

ADVENTURE

Add your images here and on the next page.

GAINING KNOWLEDGE

Add your images here and on the next page.

SPIRITUAL OR RELIGIOUS CONNECTION

Add your images here and on the next page.

PARTICIPATION IN SOCIAL ACTIVITIES AND CAUSES

Add your images here and on the next page.

ANYTHING ELSE?

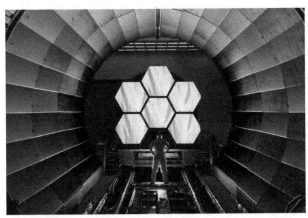

Add your images here and on the next page.

ACTION STEPS

What I will do now to make my vision happen:

1)_____

2)_____

3)_____

4)_____

5)_____

6)_____

7)_____

8)_____

9)_____

10)_____

ADDITIONAL COMMENTS

MY CONTACT INFORMATION

_____

_____

_____

_____

_____

ABOUT THE AUTHOR

GINI GRAHAM SCOTT, Ph.D., J.D., is a nationally known writer, consultant, speaker, and seminar leader, specializing in business and work relationships, professional and personal development, social trends, and popular culture. She has published over 50 books with major publishers. She has worked with dozens of clients on memoirs, self-help, popular business books, and film scripts. Writing samples are at www.ginigrahamscott.com and www.changemakerspublishingandwriting.com. She is a Huffington Post regular columnist, commenting on social trends, business, and everyday life at www.huffingtonpost.com/gini-graham-scott.

She is the founder of Changemakers Publishing, featuring books on work, business, psychology, social trends, and self-help. It has published over 50 print, e-books, and audiobooks. She has licensed several dozen books for foreign sales, including the UK, Russia, Korea, Spain, and Japan.

She has received national media exposure for her books, including appearances on *Good Morning America, Oprah,* and *CNN.* She has been the producer and host of a talk show series, *Changemakers*, featuring interviews on social trends.

Her books on business relationships and professional development include:
Turn Your Dreams into Reality (Llewellyn)
Resolving Conflict (Changemakers Publishing)
A Survival Guide for Working with Bad Bosses (AMACOM)
A Survival Guide for Working with Humans (AMACOM)
Credit Card Fraud with Jen Grondahl Lee (Rowman)
Lies and Liars: How and Why Sociopaths Lie (Skyhorse Publishing)

Scott is also active in a number of community and business groups, including the Lafayette, Pleasant Hill, and Danville Chambers of Commerce. She is a graduate of the prestigious Leadership Contra Costa program, is a member of two B2B groups in Danville and Walnut Creek, and a BNI member. She is the organizer of six Meetup groups in the film and publishing industries with over 5000 members in Los Angeles and the San Francisco Bay Area. She does workshops and seminars on the topics of her books.

She received her Ph.D. from the University of California, Berkeley, and her J.D. from the University of San Francisco Law School. She has received several MAs at Cal State University, East Bay.

CHANGEMAKERS PUBLISHING
3527 Mt. Diablo Blvd., #273
Lafayette, CA 94549
changemakers@pacbell.net . (925) 385-0608
www.changemakerspublishingandwriting.com

CPSIA information can be obtained
at www.ICGtesting.com
Printed in the USA
LVHW061545230520
656346LV00012B/738